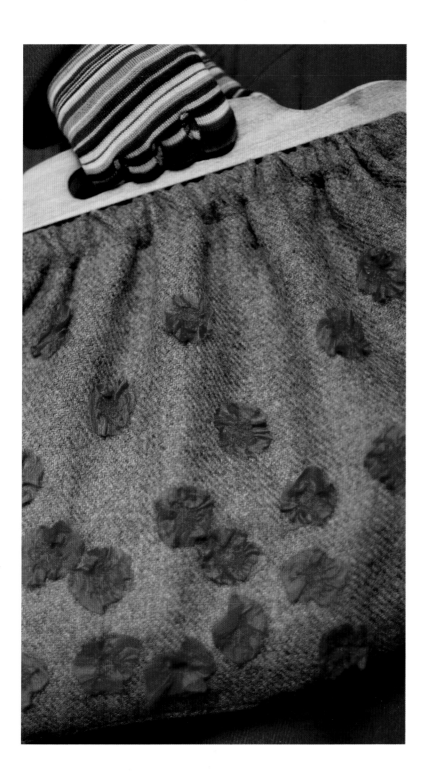

simply

needlefelt

simply needlefelt

20 EASY AND ELEGANT DESIGNS

JAYNE EMERSON

INTERWEAVE
interweavebooks.com

interweavebooks.com

First published in North America by
Interweave Press, LLC
201 East Fourth Street
Loveland, CO 80537
interweavebooks.com

Created, designed, and edited by
Berry & Co (Publishing) Ltd
47 Crewys Road
Child's Hill, London NW2 2AU

Editor Susan Berry
Designer Anne Wilson
Proofreader and indexer Katie Hardwicke
Project photography John Heseltine
Step and alternatives photography Luke Brason
Stylists Susan Berry and Jayne Emerson
Diagrams and illustrations Ed Berry

Printed in China by Asia Pacific Offset.

Library of Congress Cataloging-in-Publication Data

Emerson, Jayne.
 Simply needlefelt : 20 easy and elegant designs /
Jayne Emerson,
author.
  p. cm.
 Includes index.
 ISBN 978-1-59668-108-8
 1. Embroidery. 2. Felt work. I. Title.
TT770.E5154 2009
746.44--dc22
                    2008049160

10 9 8 7 6 5 4 3 2 1

contents

introduction

If you look closely at commercially-made felt squares you will see thousands of little holes in the fabric surface. This is because many non-woven fabrics are made by needle felting. Large, industrial machines with many hundreds of barbed needles punch through fibers that are arranged in a web and entangle them into what you see as felt fabric.

Traditionally, when felt is made in a domestic or craft environment it is done by wet felting. For large pieces, this is a relatively quick and enjoyable way of producing felt. Needle felting is a dry process, sometimes called dry felting, that allows for much greater precision. You can choose a particular area you want to felt and use the technique to create controled embellishments, texture, and color. As well as showing you the basics of needle felting, I have chosen to explore ways to create exciting modern textiles using the needle-felting process. My favorite results are the modern needle-felted weaves and the textured knits.

Fiber artists use needle felting to produce wonderfully intricate sculpted forms and there are many books that concentrate on this technique. In this book I merely touch on this subject, in the forms of jewelry and buttons, as I preferred instead to explore the use of needle felting in producing extraordinary fabric effects.

As a textile designer, the idea of creating textural and decorative embellishments without actually threading a needle is incredibly exciting. Needle-punch (embellisher) machines are becoming increasingly popular and make light work of large needle-felted projects and very quick work of smaller ones. The hand tools (both single and multineedle) now available may not be so quick but they make needle felting a brilliantly portable craft, although you need to be careful to give it your full concentration as the needles are incredibly sharp.

I am aware that not everyone will own a needle-punch machine and also that some people prefer to work by hand, so I have tried to ensure that most of the projects in this book can be worked either way.

When designing, you need to establish a theme and color palette. I like to gather ideas from magazines and photographs to create a mood board (right). The images do not necessarily need to be needle-felted, but they do need to be inspiring.

tools and equipment

You don't need a needle-punch machine to complete the projects in this book as they can all be done by hand, but if the needle-felting bug takes hold of you, a machine will be high on your wish list. I find that a single-needle hand tool is best for finer decorative embellishments and 3-D forms. A multineedle hand tool (specifically the Clover tool) is particularly useful as its five needles considerably speed up the needle-felting process. I often use this tool to lightly needle-felt a design in position before finishing it off on the machine. The needle-punch machine is basically a motorized version of the multineedle hand tool and speeds up the whole process even further. The machine is excellent for larger projects and for completing smaller ones at lightning speed, but you can decide which process suits you best.

hand tools

Needles

The needles are barbed, which means that they have tiny notches cut in their sides that catch and entangle fibers. They come in different gauges so you can choose your needle size as you would a sewing-machine needle to suit the fiber or fabric you will be working on. The higher the gauge, the finer the needle, though sometimes you may want to use a really thick needle on a fine fabric if your aim is to distort it and add texture. The needles are made from stainless steel and are very sharp; they easily break if bent. Needles can be used individually for fine detailing with or without a wooden handle. Alternatively they can be used collectively to needle-felt larger areas either in a multineedle wooden handle or the Clover tool (below).

Foam mat

When you needle-felt with a hand tool the needles are pushed or punched through the layers of fiber or fabric from top to bottom, so you need a base into which the needles can safely plunge. Styrofoam or dense sponge are good options for such a base when working with a single-needle tool as they provide a firm base on which to sculpt forms or work fine detailing.

> **TIP**
>
> **If you want to make a larger piece of felt, use a corresponding size piece of foam as a base. However, as a general rule I would use traditional wet felting for larger pieces.**

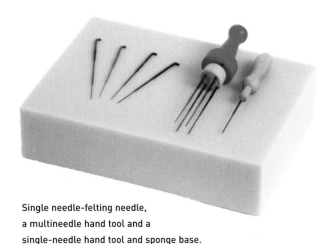

Single needle-felting needle, a multineedle hand tool and a single-needle hand tool and sponge base.

The Clover multineedle tool with two sizes of brush mat used with the Clover tool.

Clover felting tool

I have found this tool to be the best hand alternative to the needle-punch machine and ideal for decorative embellishment. It has five needles. These operate using a spring mechanism, which makes hand punching quick and relatively effortless. It has the benefit of a plastic guard around the needles to help protect your fingers.

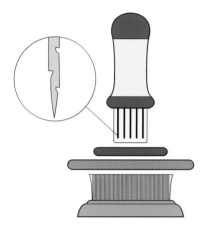

This diagram shows how the multineedle tool operates.

Brush mat

This is used with the Clover felting tool. The mat is like a stiff brush with a hard plastic base (opposite page). It's really nice to felt into because the bristles provide a perfect base that doesn't become "felted" to your work!

If you use regular-length felting needles with this base make sure you do not stab the needles so deeply that they hit the plastic base.

machine tools

Needle-punch machine

This looks very like a sewing machine, but there is no thread and no bobbin, just a collection of barbed needles. It works on the same principle as hand needle-felting but makes the whole process a lot quicker.

Machine needle-felting is similar to free-motion machine embroidery in that the machine does not feed the fabric; instead you have to move the fabric around yourself. This may take a bit of practice, but at least there are no bobbins, tension, or thread to worry about. The speed at which you run the machine—using the presser foot coupled with your fabric movement—will determine the degree of felting on each area of your work. Move your fabric smoothly and avoid pulling it to prevent the needles from breaking. Depending on the thickness of the work, the foot should be adjusted as low as it will go to avoid unnecessary pulling.

Machine-finished needle felting tends to be a lot flatter than hand-finished needle felting with the underside fibers meshed at a shallower, more uniform depth.

Below, a typical needle-punch machine with a close-up (below) of the needles and needleguard. The foot adjustment (low, medium, or high) can be seen on the right of the picture.

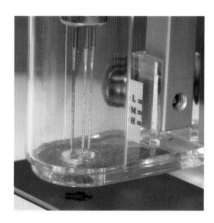

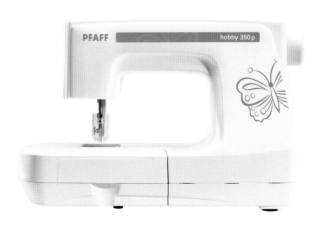

useful equipment and materials

Water-soluble fabric

This provides a good base to work upon when creating felt fabric from scratch and is essential when working with fleece using a needle-punch machine. It dissolves in water, but you can limit the amount you decide to wash away. If you want to create soft felt then you need to wash away all the water-soluble fabric. I often choose to wash only part of the fabric away, producing a dry felt with a more rigid structure. This technique is great for making vessels and boxes.

Cutting mat and rotary cutter with a variety of blades

Part of the appeal of felted fabrics is that you don't have to hem them. For a long time now I have used a rotary cutter to achieve pristine straight edges on pattern pieces and then discovered that the blades also come in wavy, zigzag, and perforated forms. It is such an easy way of finishing your work, but the effects can make a simple item look stunning.

Tailor's chalk pencils and water-soluble marker pens

These provide the simplest way to transfer a design to your fabric by drawing the design with the chalk or marker freehand or tracing around a pattern or template. The marks can be removed easily by brushing away chalk marks or soaking the fabric in water in the case of water-soluble pens.

Fabric adhesive spray

I have a tendency to reach for the fabric adhesive spray with everything I do, as it is so quick and easy. I will often position yarns and fabric, spray them in place, and then needle-felt the design only when I am entirely satisfied with the arrangement. This works well, but do remember that during the needle-felting process fibers shrink and this can create problems on larger designs.

General sewing kit

You will need good-quality dressmakers' scissors, small embroidery scissors, general purpose sewing needles and thread, and a tape measure.

It is a good idea to keep all your equipment in a workbag or box, as the felting needles are sharp. Keep the bag or box out of the reach of small children.

Paper for patterns and templates

Sheets of A4 paper and tracing paper are useful for copying designs for paper patterns and for creating the templates. You will need a pen or pencil, too.

Making paper templates

A few projects require paper templates. You will need paper or card, a pen or pencil, and some sharp scissors as well as tracing paper if you want to copy a design from which to create a template. The templates used in this book are shown on pages 106 to 107.

yarns, fleece, and fabric

The obvious choice of materials for needle felting is unspun fleeces, as they felt so easily. However, I love to experiment with all types of fabrics and yarns, even with those that you might think would not work at all. The way that fabrics and fibers react is all part of the fun. Wool fiber is the staple ingredient as the natural scales on the fiber strands allow them to mat together easily when felted. Artificial smooth fibers are at the other end of the spectrum—they will hardly felt at all. However, some fabrics, like silk chiffon, will ruche and pucker when needle-felted to other fabrics, creating really interesting textures as they do so.

I am always in pursuit of beautiful happy accidents, but I do tend to break a few needles along the way. Feathers, metalic yarns, beads, and sequins have all caused needles to break in the past and should therefore be used in needle felting with caution.

Fleece

Carded and combed, but unspun,100% wool fleece, also known as wool tops, usually comes from Merino sheep and is traditionally used in wet feltmaking. It is a staple ingredient for making felt, 3-D forms, and creating decorative embellishment on a background fabric, as well as binding nonfibrous fabrics together.

Spun yarns

The more loosely spun and fibrous the yarn, the easier it is to use. Bouclés, fancy yarns, thick, and fine wools can all be used. Chunky 100% wool yarn is specially good as it needle-felts almost as easily as fleece.

Felt

Commercially-made felt is an ideal background for appliqué; the slightly thicker wool-based felts tend to pucker less than the cheaper synthetic varieties.

Wool fabrics

Wool sweaters that have shrunk in the wash, felted weaves, and even traditional tweeds all work well as a background fabric. Look for 100% wool cloth—the more fibrous the better.

Organza, chiffon, silk

These are tricky. I stand in the fabric store wishing I had my needles on hand to try out a sample. They are generally used for creating texture, as the needles pucker, ruche, and gather these fabrics. Generally polyester and silk organzas work brilliantly as do plain weave silks. It is best to buy old garments and scarves from thrift stores so that if the fabric doesn't work it is no great loss.

Denim

Look out for deep blue or black thick denims. The wrong side should show a white weave so that when needle-felted on this side, the white fibers transfer to the front, creating an attractive, distressed look.

Net

Interesting effects can be produced by securing delicate nonfibrous fabrics to a more fibrous fabric, with the aid of a little fleece or a very fibrous fabric. Any non-fibrous fabric can be attached to another fabric using this technique, but lightweight nets create some surprisingly ethereal effects that you do not usually see in needle-felted items.

basic techniques

Needle-felting simply involves the meshing together of fibers with the use of barbed needles. The principle is the same whether you use a single-needle hand tool, a multineedle tool, or a machine, though with the hand tools you will need something to punch into—either a brush mat or a sponge. The needles are punched into the fibers repeatedly and, as they punch, the barbs on the needles tangle and amalgamate the fibers, forming a firm bond. This bond can take the form of basic felt, embellishments, or appliqué. Once you have mastered the basic principles of needle felting you can begin to understand the design possibilities and the fun that you can have. The idea that you can just felt sections of a fabric, add detailed embellishments, or make simple felt flowers is mesmerizing.

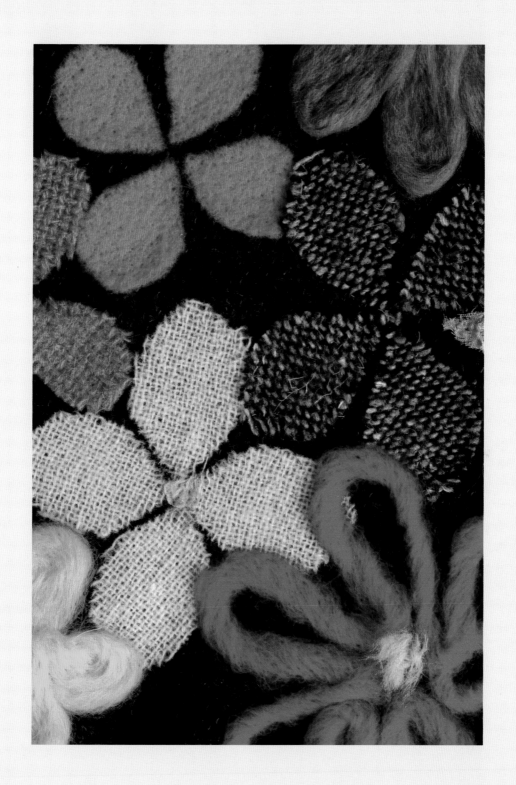

basic dry felting

Felt fabric can be made from pure wool fleece using either the hand or machine needle-felting technique. The basic principle is similar to traditional wet felting as the fleece fibers are laid down in layers, each layer laid crosswise on top of the previous layer. In needle felting, however, it is the punching action of the needles that amalgamates the fibers rather than soapy water and rubbing as in wet felting. To hand needle-felt a large piece would take much longer than wet felting but the benefit of needle felting is that you have so much more control when blending colors and adding details. Precise embellishments and motifs can be worked into the felt as it is being made with no fear that the agitation and rubbing will move and distort them.

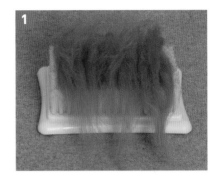

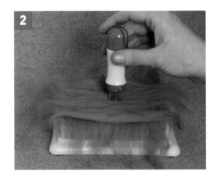

hand needle-felting

When needle-felting pure wool fleece, the thickness of the final felt fabric is determined by the number of layers of fleece laid down. Three to four layers will usually suffice.

1 Tease out the tufts of fleece so that each is about 4" (10cm) long. Place the brush or Styrofoam base on a work surface. Lay the tufts of teased fleece across the brush or sponge base in one direction only.

2 Now add a second layer of tufts of fleece, but in the opposite direction to the first layer, as shown. Felt the fibers by punching all over the surface area with the hand tool (a Clover tool is used here). Keep the tool vertical to prevent the needles from breaking.

3 Fold in any stray fibers from the sides as you go. The more you punch the fibers, the more felted they will become.

4 Lift the fleece from the mat periodically to stop it from getting felted to the mat. Hold the felt up to the light to check for any thin areas, and add more fleece if needed. Keep felting until the desired thickness is achieved.

machine needle-felting

In order to make felt using a needle-punch machine you must have some way of containing the fibers. Water-soluble fabric is perfect for this and has the added bonus that, should you wish to felt a specific shape, the design can be drawn onto it first as a guide.

Remember to keep the fabric moving as you machine, as needle-felting in one place for too long will result in holes forming, as the fibers begin to break down completely.

As with the hand tool, various needle gauges can be bought for the machine. The thicker gauges are great for heavier fabrics but leave larger holes in the surface of your fabric; finer gauges are preferable for finer fibers.

If the work has a few holes, this can often be rectified by lightly punching the fibers again with finer needles.

1 Tease out the tufts of fleece and lay them on a base of water-soluble fabric (see Steps 1 and 2, left).

2 Needle-felt by machine and smooth down the fibers as you work. Lightly needle-felt all over the surface area at first, then work over it again until all the fibers are meshed together.

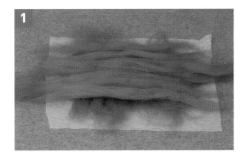

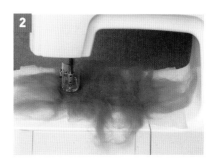

3 As with the hand tool, you can fold the surplus fibers into your felt as you work or simply trim them off later. Remember to hold the felt up to the light occasionally to check that the density of your felt is uniform all over. At this stage you can add more fibers to any areas that require it and needle felt again.

4 When satisfied that the fibers are evenly felted, immerse the piece in water to dissolve the water-soluble fabric. Wrap the felt in a towel to remove any excess water and then leave in a warm place to dry.

Don't waste your felt!

You can use your practice pieces of felt as a base and embellish the surface with yarns, fabric, or further fleece motifs. Alternatively you could cut the felt into a shape and use it on its own or as an appliqué. Felt shapes can also be made by following a drawn design on water-soluble fabric (see Felt Flowers, page 40).

embellishing fleece

Fleece is probably the best material with which to produce really fine detailing. You can create these embellishments either freehand or by drawing your design first onto the fabric using chalk or a fabric-marker pen. By twisting, rolling, and tucking the fibers back on themselves, beautiful effects can be produced. You can choose to use very thin quantities of fleece for wispy, almost translucent effects or lots of fleece so as to build up the fibers until the felt is opaque and almost 3-D in effect. Choose the appropriate tool; intricate areas will require a single needle, but larger areas can be started by hand and finished on a machine.

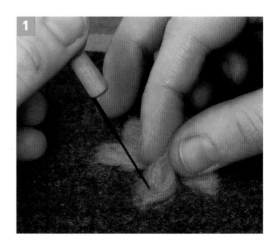

fleece flowers

A flower is a good place to start when learning how to apply fleece.

Needle-felting petals

1 Take a small amount of fleece, fold it in half, then twist the folded end. Needle-felt in the desired position. If you needle-felt all around the edge of the drawn petal shape, any stray fibers can be pushed into the work with the needle. To create a rounded edge, just fold the fleece and needle-felt in position.

Needle-felting dots

2 Roll a small amount of fleece between your fingers or your palms, then needle-felt this onto the flower at its center, using a single-needle tool, before working around the edges, gathering in any loose fibers as you go.

Needle-felting stems or fine lines

3 Twist a small amount of fleece to form a line. Needle-felt in position with a single-needle tool. Tuck the end of the fleece back on itself if you want a clean end.

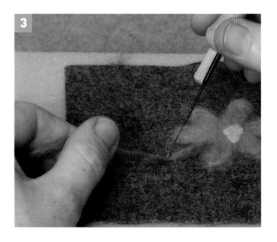

alternative embellishments

Here are some simple ways to make little decorative additions using texture and color to enliven a basic design.

Making thin wisps

1 Tease out very fine lengths of fleece and needle-felt them to a background fabric. You can then add wisp-like effects to create atmospheric detail in a design.

Making tufts

2 Cut little tufts of fleece with scissors to give sharper detailing. I made these by taking a small wisp of fleece, folding it in half and then cutting the folded ends. I then gave the fold a little twist and needle-felted it to the fabric with a single-needle tool.

Twisting colors

3 Loosely twist two or more colors of fleece together and needle-felt them in place using a multineedle tool. They look particularly good when coiled to form a circle as shown in Step 3. (This technique also works well when the fleeces are braided.)

TIPS

- You can also build up layers of fleece on fabric and create 3-D embellishments that can then be sculpted using a single-needle hand tool. The basic principles can be found on page 22.

- For inspiration on embellishing with fleece turn to pages 66 to 67 and look at the alternative samples.

using templates

You can use this basic technique to make felt shapes with or without a background fabric. A simple paper pattern can be used as a template, but you could employ any chosen shape.

1 Tease out some tufts of fleece and lay them on your background fabric (or directly onto the mat if you are simply making a felt shape). Lay down enough fleece so that it can be seen all around the edges of your paper pattern.

2 Using a single-needle tool, punch all around the outline of the paper pattern.

3 Remove the pattern and fold the excess fleece into the design. The punched line will hold the fleece down and define the shape. Once you have folded all the excess fleece in, you can needle-felt the design firmly in place using a multineedle tool or the needle-punch machine.

4 Use the shape or shapes for appliqué!

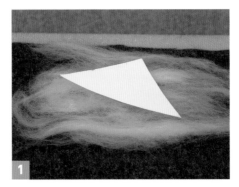

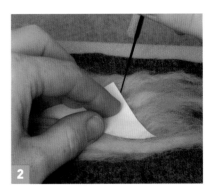

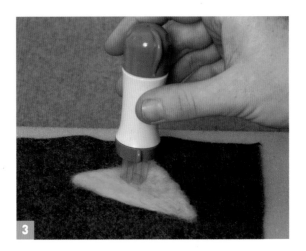

Creating felt shapes

You could use a plastic mold such as a cookie cutter to create individual felt shapes. In this case, the fleeces are simply laid down in the mold in the usual crosswise layers and then needle-felted by hand, as shown on page 75. You could use this technique for making raised motifs that are almost 3-D in shape.

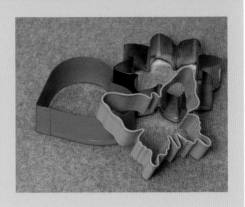

blending colors

Really interesting effects can be obtained by blending different colors of fleece before you embark on the felting process. You can either finely blend the fleece to create entirely new colors or loosely blend it to gain a striped or marbled effect.

1 Pull off tufts of fleece about 4" (10cm) long and blend them together.

2 Make your felt in the usual way, following Steps 1 to 4 of Hand Needle-felting on page 16.

3 Use the felt as a base for further embellishment or cut it into your chosen shape.

4 Then use it for appliqué!

Steps 1 to 4 of Hand Needle-felting on page 16.

NEEDLE-FELTING TIPS

- Always needle-felt onto a brush mat or piece of foam.

- Always stab the needle vertically into the fabric to avoid breakages.

- Do not over needle-felt or you will eventually destroy the fibers altogether and end up with a hole!

- Decide which side of the fabric will be the "right" side, and don't push any unwanted fibers through from the "wrong" side.

- Keep fingers out of the way as the needles are very sharp and barbed.

- Test the chosen techniques on a variety of fabrics to check the possible results.

- Store the needles safely when not in use.

- When needle-felting by hand, lift the fabric periodically to avoid it becoming attached to the mat.

- If you own a needle-punch machine, start work off with a hand tool first to "baste" your design in place.

- The more you felt, the more the original yarn or fabric will shrink.

3-D and sculpted forms

The art of creating needle-felted forms has been used by fiber artists for many years. Amazingly detailed sculptures are cleverly crafted from fleece, often with the aid of a single needle. I am not making anything ambitious in this book; I am just offering a very basic introduction.

The principle is interesting because it can be used in simple jewelry and for 3-D embellishments on fabric. And needle felting allows you to be really precise when creating these forms.

Sculpted felt techniques are best worked on a Styrofoam or dense sponge base with a single-needle tool. Wooden handles can be obtained that make the needle easier to hold, but an elastic band wrapped tightly around the top of the shaft will also prevent your fingers from slipping.

3-D shapes

Basic shapes can all be made in this way. Most fiber artists will make simple shapes then needle-felt them together to form more complex forms.

1 Take a small tuft of fleece and roll it tightly to form an oval-shaped ball.

2 Roll the emerging shape around the mat, needle-felting all the time. Do not cut any surplus fleece away from the form but tear the remaining fibers away as these will blend more easily than a cut edge.

3 Keep rolling the fleece around the mat, needle-felting as you go, until you are happy with the shape. Add more fleece if necessary by wrapping it around the ball and continuing to needle-felt as you do so.

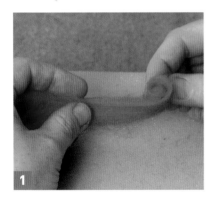

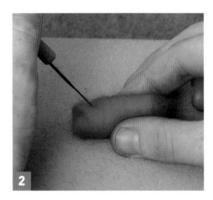

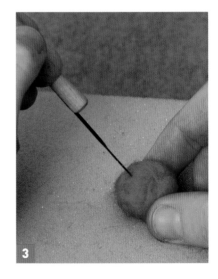

sculpting with the needle

Needle-felting continuously in one place with a single needle will form indentations in the form, which allows for further detailing in the sculpting process. Fiber artists use this technique to great effect to create intricate detailing, but I am just going to show you the basics by making a simple heart shape.

1 Prepare some 4" (10cm) tufts of red fleece, remembering that the fleece will shrink as you felt it, so you will need twice the volume of your planned finished shape.

2 Start to needle-felt with a single-needle tool to mesh the fibers, adding more layers of fleece if you need them. Keep folding the fibers in on themselves and constantly turn the fleece as you needle-felt.

3 When the fibers start to nicely mesh together you can begin to form your heart shape. Twist the bottom of the heart to form a point and needle-felt it to hold this shape. Now start to make the top indentation of the heart by continuously needle-felting in a small, straight line.

4 Continue until you have created the complete indentation for the top of the heart.

5 Turn into a necklace or earrings.

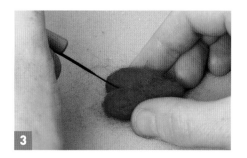

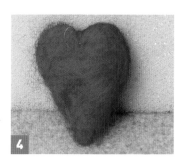

TIP
You can use this technique to make a variety of different shapes, such as cylinders, squares, and so on, and use them combined with circular shapes, or with beads, for a necklace or bracelet (see page 44).

appliqué needle felting

Many different fibers, fabrics, and yarns can be applied to a background fabric, each producing a different effect. During the needle-felting process the fibers are pulled through to the wrong side of the work entangling themselves as they go and fastening the appliqué in place. Because the needles pull out of the work smoothly, the underside of the work is left with a fibrous shadow. A hand tool will create a more prominent fiber buildup, depending on how deep you stab the needle or needles. Indeed, sometimes the surprise is that the back of your work is more interesting and subtler than the front.

If you felt both sides of the fabric, the fibers from the back (including fibers from the background fabric) will get pushed through to the front of your work. Different techniques call for one-sided or double-sided needle felting, but as a rule, if you want one fiber to adhere to another without changing its color or texture too much, you should only needle-felt the side you are working on. Some fibers, such as silk, will pucker and ruche when punched with the felting needles because the barbs snag the threads, pulling and distorting the weave.

felt appliqué

This simple bird silhouette was cut from a piece of commercially-made black felt. It has been needle-felted onto thick cream wool cloth to demonstrate just how effective felt appliqué can be. I like the fact that there is no stitching to distract from the simplicity of the motif and that the design looks just as good on the back of the fabric as it does on the front.

1 Place your background fabric on the brush mat or foam base. Position the appliqué on the background fabric, and lightly punch the needle through all the layers all over the whole design to "baste" in position. At this stage it is very easy to remove and readjust your design.

2 Once you are happy with your design position, needle-felt using either a multineedle tool or the needle-punch machine until the design is firmly in position.

3 The back of the work is often as interesting as the front. This pic shows the reverse side of the appliqué. The amount and length of fiber show-through will depend on how many times you punch, how many needles you use, whether you use a hand tool or the machine and, in the case of hand tools, how far through the fabric you push the needles.

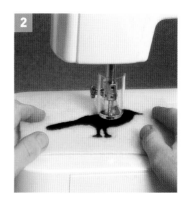

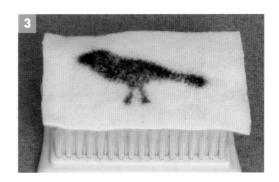

needle-felting couched yarns

Yarn can be used as an outline or a design in itself. Multiple colors can also be twisted or braided together and then needle-felted.

1 Lay the background fabric on the mat and then loosely lay the yarn in the desired position. Baste the yarn in position with a few punches of a multineedle tool, being careful not to stretch the yarn. Continue until your design is in place; you can easily reposition it at this stage.

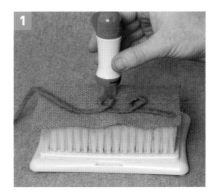

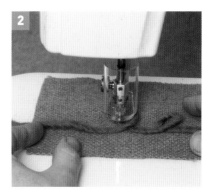

2 Needle-felt in place using either a multi-needle hand tool or the machine. The more you punch, the more the yarn will mesh and felt into the foundation fabric.

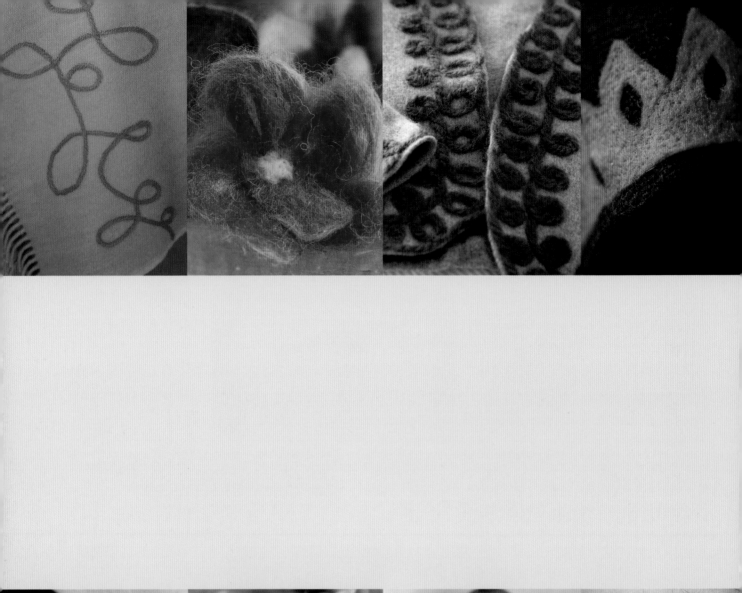

projects

fabric appliqué

This form of appliqué is entirely stitch-free! The absence of stitch lines means that motifs and designs applied in this way look clean and uncluttered. All the appliqués in this chapter are really simple. If you are lucky enough to be able to draw well you can get carried away with beautiful freehand designs. If, like me, you are always looking for new ways to design without drawing, you will love the simplicity of using paper-cut templates. I remember first trying this technique at an after-school club when I was about eight. The streams of snowflakes and paper chains we created look pretty good when transposed into needle-felted designs.

Different fabrics give very different results and store-bought felt is probably the best fabric to begin experimenting with as the appliqué needle-felts perfectly to it. Once you move on to silks and organdies (see pages 88 to 95), you create added textures with puckering and fraying. Even the size needle you choose will affect the surface texture of the end result. It comes down to experimentation and the effect you want to achieve.

snowflake table runner

I have a lot of vintage sewing books in my studio and while I was writing this book I discovered I had one dating from 1965, called *Discovering Embroidery* by Winsome Douglas ... what a fantastic name! In it, she suggests using folded, paper-cut templates for designs. I loved the idea of incorporating this idea into a needle-felt project, as it is a brilliant way to produce great shapes without the need for drawing skills.

This table runner was inspired by a retro coffee table that has tiles inlaid in the top. In my design, I love the way the bright orange sings out from the subtle tweed. The combination of fabric is great as the felt fibers blend easily with the tweed, giving the fabric the look of flocked wallpaper. It would be perfect for a retro bachelor pad.

You will need

- Length of felted wool tweed to suit chosen table. Mine was 62" x 17" (155 x 43cm)
- 6 squares of orange felt (12"/30cm square)
- Piece of paper (8¼"/21cm square)
- Felt-tip pen
- Scissors
- Fabric adhesive spray

Making the runner

1 Cut out your base fabric to the appropriate size. If you want to duplicate the appliqué pattern size, use the same width that I have. Hem the edges by zigzag stitching the raw edges all around and then folding under a ¾" (1.5cm) hem. Machine stitch to secure.

2 Make the snowflake template by folding a square of paper in half, then in half again, and finally diagonally across. Draw your pattern (copy my template on page 107) and then cut it out.

3 Pin or lightly spray glue onto the right side of the chosen fabric, such as the felt used here. Cut out six snowflakes—three at each end of the runner—if you want to follow my design.

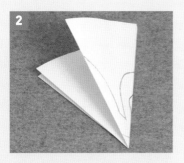

4 Place your felt patterns (main and scraps) at one end of your tweed fabric (following the layout shown in the main picture, page 30) and lightly spray with adhesive. You can use scraps of felt to highlight the design. Needle-felt lightly in place with a hand tool. Repeat at the other end.

5 When you are happy with your design, finish off the needle-felting (either by hand or machine) so that all the shapes are firmly secured.

TIP

When making a paper pattern, remember that cuts in the folds will produce a more intricately detailed pattern. Cutting across the central corner of all the folds will make a central hole. When cutting out the pattern in the chosen fabric, keep any small scraps to highlight your design.

border design

I have created this version of the paper-cut design for a border using a commercially-made felt on a simple black skirt. When you needle-felt your border to the base fabric you will effectively seal any raw edges, so you won't need to hem the base fabric, although, in this case, the skirt already had its own hem. You can experiment with this idea for an edging design for a bolero (see Needle-felted Knits, page 102).

You can make your own paper-cut patterns very easily. Any repeating small image will work very well. You don't have to be precise in your drawing for the paper pattern. It is more charming if slightly irregular and "handmade."

Size

The depth of the border is 2″ (5cm)

You will need

- A4 paper for pattern
- Felt-tip pen
- Scissors
- Felt fabric for border
- Fabric marking pencil

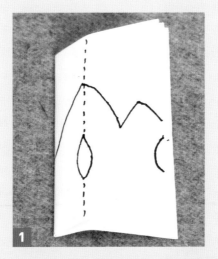

Making the paper pattern

1 Cut a strip of paper from the length of your A4 sheet that is at least 3″ (8cm) wide. Fold in half, in half again, and in half yet again. Draw your border outline on the top of the folded paper in a felt-tip pen (or trace the template on page 107). If you want to make holes in the design, as I have, then fold in half again and make another cut in this fold (see dotted line in picture).

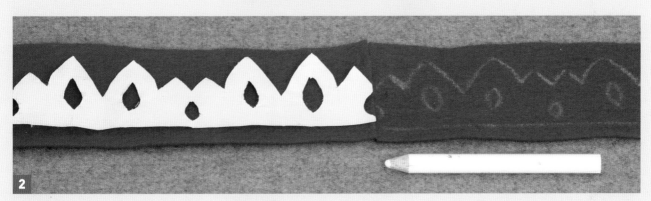

TIP

If you are using squares of felt rather than a length as I did here, you will need to cut the border out in sections. To disguise the joins, slightly overlap the edges as you needle-felt. The felting process will merge the fibers and you will barely notice them by the time the skirt is finished!

Creating the border

2 Cut out the paper template and lay it on your chosen border fabric, marking the outline with a fabric marking pencil. Move the paper template along to create the length of border you want. Then cut out the border lengths.

3 Position the border on the base fabric and "baste" it in position by lightly needle-felting with a hand tool. Then needle-felt it securely with a multineedle hand tool or a needle-punch machine.

floral cards

For this card I used paper originally designed for acrylic paints. Its interesting surface texture makes a great background for any little masterpieces of textured needle felting. Making similarly small items with simple motifs is a great way to experiment with different fabrics while creating a stash of beautiful homemade cards.

A basic flower design will provide you with a greetings card for any occasion but why not try other motifs? A needle-felted heart (see page 23) for Valentine's day, a simple house for a "welcome to your new home," or even basic numbers for a child's birthday.

Size

The card is 5" x 7" (23 x 17.5cm)

You will need

- Scraps of various fabrics (black felt, white and yellow silks)
- Sheet of acrylic 300gsm card 10" x 7" (25 x 17.5cm)
- Felt-tip pen
- Scissors
- Ruler and craft knife
- Double-sided Sellotape

Making the petals

1 Fold the white silk into quarters, then fold again to form eight layers. Press lightly with an iron. Draw around a paper petal template (see page 106), onto the fabric four times. Cut out 28 petals.

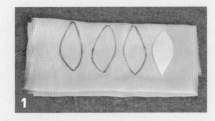

2 Discard the top petals, with the drawn line. Build up a flower shape with the petal as shown and start to needle-felt them lightly to the base fabric by hand. Once they are all in position, needle-felt them more securely either by hand or by machine.

3 Add a little scrap of yellow silk to the center of your flower and needle-felt in position using a hand tool as this allows for greater precision in its placement.

TIPS

- Never be tempted to use glue as it has a nasty habit of soaking through your fabric and ruining your work.

- A rotary cutter and cutting mat are helpful when a design demands precise squares and straight lines.

- Don't be tempted to needle-felt too much. If you do, the barbed needles will eventually destroy the fibers completely, leaving you with holes in your work.

Making the card

4 Take your sheet of acrylic card and score it lightly down the center with a knife blade, then fold to form the card.

5 Cut your needle-felted flower fabric into a square or a rectangle.

6 Fix the flower to the card using double-sided Sellotape.

alternative flower designs

Here are some additional flower designs you might like to use, whether for a little card or as appliqués on garments. The designs I show here use a variety of fabrics—for example flowers cut from an old silk scarf and needle-felted to a knitted cashmere base fabric—but you can experiment with the fabrics that appeal most to you.

Really interesting effects are created when you needle-felt heavier weight fabrics to a lighter weight base, such as cotton voile, for example.

Your color choices can be subtle or bold, mono-chromatic, or multicolored. Needle-felting different fabrics in toning colors creates more emphasis on the texture.

Repeat designs on a larger scale probably requires a needle-punch machine unless you are very patient!

Sometimes the reverse effects are even more interesting (see pages 78 to 87).

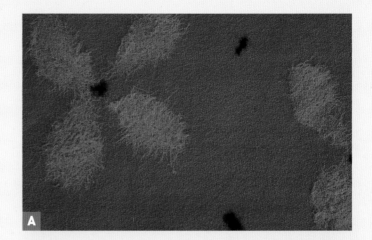

A Silk chiffon becomes a tangled mass of fibers when needle-felted to a dark orange wool crepe. Tiny scraps of black silk Dupioni create the polka dot design.

B Miniature pansies have been cut from a vintage floral silk scarf and applied to baby-blue woven cashmere fabric. I really like the fact that you can see the tiny holes made by the needles, as if they were embroidered with invisible thread!

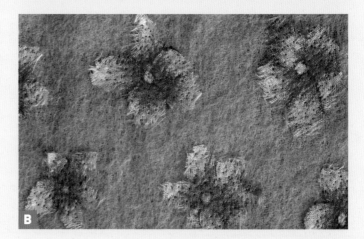

C Multicolored silk floral fabric transforms itself into beautiful blurry petals when needle-felted onto silk voile. Little scraps of yellow damask make up the centers.

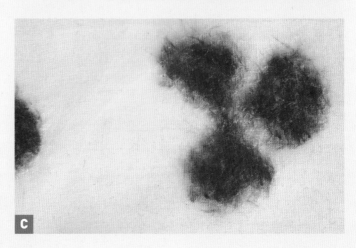

D I cut these chiffon roses from a cheap polyester scarf I found in a thrift store, and I then needle-felted them to heavy black silk. Needle-felting the entire sample, rather than just the flowers, created even more texture.

E Cotton flannel makes a great backing fabric to which to apply silks. I used a ditzy floral silk that distorted as it was punched into the cotton. The back of this one (below) has an attractively softened effect too.

F In this sample I experimented with flowers cut from a piece of floral wool fabric and needle-felted them to black felt. The fibers didn't break up as easily as those in silk but I like the way the edges frayed while the body of the flower remained almost unchanged.

3-D felt

Needle-felting is the perfect way to make colorful, sculpted felt. Some fleece, a single needle, and a foam mat are all that is required to make a 3-D felted shape. Once you get the hang of making the simple felt shapes shown in this chapter, you can move on to making more detailed forms either for jewelry making or as sculptures in their own right.

This book is mostly about embellishing fabrics so I have merely touched on the subject of 3-D felt in this section. There are some fantastic books specializing in this subject with outstanding results, but they are not my forte as they are a bit too fiddly and intricate.

I have limited myself in this chapter to making different versions of felt flowers and some simple jewelry. Both give endless opportunites for variations on a basic theme, which is within any novice needle-felter's grasp.

felt flowers

Small pieces of flat felt can incorporate colorful details added either during the felt-making process or as embellishments once the felt is made. Water-soluble fabric is a brilliant surface to work upon. Not only does it provide a stable surface but you can also draw the outline of the shape of the felt that you want to produce. Another benefit is that you can vary the amount of water-soluble fabric that you wash away after the felting is complete. If you allow a little of the water-soluble fabric to remain in the felt, it will be slightly firmer and can then be used for objects that require more structure. These felt flowers are a perfect way to begin experimenting. You can use them in many ways. I have shown a flower and leaves (page 41) as a decoration to a parcel, but you could turn one into a brooch by adding a brooch back or attaching one or more to hair clips or hats.

Size

Flower measures about 3" (8cm) in diameter

You will need

- Small amounts of various colors of fleece
- Water-soluble fabric
- Fabric marking pencil

Making a flower

1 Cut a piece of water-soluble fabric and draw or trace the flower shape from page 106. Tease out tufts of fleece and form into a petal shape by taking a tuft of fleece and folding it in half so the folded end becomes the petal edge. Needle-felt with a single-needle tool using the drawn outline as a guide.

2 Use tiny amounts of other colors of fleece in a similar way, but laying each new color on top of the previous one, needle-felting each layer as you go. Check the density of the felt , and needle-felt further if needed. Finally add a scrap of yellow fleece to form the center.

TIP

If you blend different colors of fleece before you start (see page 21), you can create interesting shaded effects with subtle color changes.

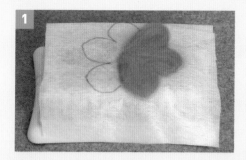

Making a leaf

3 Make the leaf in the same way, by folding some tufts of green fleece into an oblong, and then adding a line of twisted darker green fleece to form the leaf vein, before needle-felting as you did for the flower.

Finishing off the flower and leaf

4 Cut away the excess water-soluble fabric from the flower and leaf and submerge in cold water until the water-soluble fabric disappears from the edges of your flower and leaf. Allow to dry, and then trim off any stray fibers.

stemmed flowers

I wrote a book recently about machine embroidery (*The Impatient Embroiderer*) in which I included some 3-D flowers. They proved such a popular project that I thought I would make a needle-felted version in this book! As with those fabric flowers, these felted blooms are supposed to look handmade, almost like they come from fairyland. There is so much scope in needle felting to make fascinating blooms. Colors can be blended together and tiny coloration details added to the final felted petals. The edges can be left softly felted or cut to create a sharper finish. Make various sizes of flower and display in a vase.

You will need

• Selection of felt flowers and leaves from the previous project
• Fine and stiff florist's wire
• Florist's tape
• A little extra fleece in coordinating colors

Making the stems

1 Take your previously made needle-felted flower and hook a length of fine florist's wire through the center of the felt flower and then wind the two ends around an 8" to 12" (20 to 30cm) length of stiff florist's wire to form the stem.

2 Wrap florist's tape all around the stem, adding in any leaves as you go. Continue wrapping the stem until the flower head is secure.

3 Using a single-needle hand tool, carefully needle-felt more fleece into the flower center to hide any wire that may be showing.

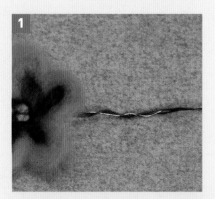

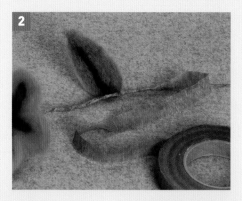

felted bead necklace

This necklace was made by taking apart an old wooden necklace and restringing it. I really like putting unexpected materials together and I think the wood, ribbon, and felt work really well here. I have been playing around with reinventing jewelry for a while now. I picked up an inexpensive set of jewelry pliers at a craft fair and have found them really useful and great fun to play with. Felted beads are now something I can add to the mix.

You will need

- Dark red fleece
- Small polystyrene balls
- Selection of large wooden beads
- ¾yd (0.75m) fine silk ribbon
- Tapestry needle
- Skewer or bradawl
- Scissors

Creating the necklace

1 Gradually wrap small tufts of fleece around a polystyrene ball needle-felting with a single-needle tool as you go, taking care to layer the fleece on evenly and making sure you cover the polystyrene base completely.

2 When the ball is covered in a firm even layer of felt, pierce the center with a skewer or bradawl to form a bead.

3 String the beads onto the ribbon using a tapestry needle, making a double knot in the ribbon before and after each bead you add.

4 Fold the ends of the ribbon in half and cut diagonally to prevent them fraying.

5 You can either tie the ribbon ends into a bow or, if you prefer, stich a button to one end and make a loop closure at the other.

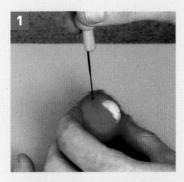

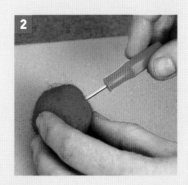

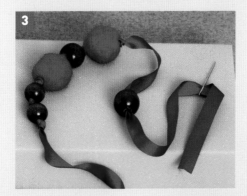

TIP

When making a necklace such as this, I find it easiest to fold the ribbon in half and start with the center bead. This means that you are left with equal amounts of ribbon on either side of the completed necklace.

swirl bracelet

This bracelet is made using two layers of colored felt. In our book, *Simply Felt*, my co-author Margaret Docherty showed how to make these swirls using wet felting. It produces such a beautiful effect that I thought I would try making them using needle felting. The initial step involves making a sheet of fleece in the chosen colors and then rolling these to form a Swiss roll shape, which is needle-felted together as one solid form.

This is then cut to produce slices of swirled colored felt. The felt slices can be used for buttons, beads, or an embellishment in their own right, which can be needle-felted onto a background fabric. I have used mine to decorate a store-bought bracelet using good quality craft glue. The plastic structure provides a sturdy base for the softer needle-felted decoration and creates a unique item of jewelry in the process.

You will need

- Black fleece
- White fleece
- Scissors
- Plastic bracelet
- Craft glue

Creating the bracelet

1 Lay down a layer of black fleece in one direction, with a second layer laid down in the opposite direction (as you would in the initial stages of making basic felt) to create a piece approximately 1" x 3" (2.5 x 8cm). Using a multineedle hand tool, needle-felt the layers together, folding in any stray fibers as you go.

2 Add two layers of white fleece, in the same way, on top of the black felt. Needle-felt together to form a two-color felt.

3 Roll the felt fabric and, holding the roll firmly in position, needle-felt until the form feels firm and solid. I find it best to start off with a single-needle hand tool and then when the roll is formed, complete with a multineedle hand tool.

4 Cut some slices from the roll. Mine measured about ¼" (0.75cm) thick.

5 Attach the felt slices to your bracelet (or your chosen fabric) using good craft glue. Allow to dry.

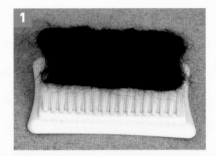

Adding colors

If you use more layers of colored fleece, your swirls will become even more colorful, and you can use them for earrings or brooches.

coasters

These coasters were inspired by an old leaflet that I found on macramé. Do you remember those knotted and coiled string projects so popular in the '70s? I have always loved the way yarn looks when it is coiled, but a coiled structure is not sufficiently interlaced so it needs a base of yarn or fleece to prevent it from falling apart.

As coasters need to be washed frequently it is a good idea to spray them with a stain-resistant medium to prevent the need for high-temperature washing, which would cause further felting to occur.

Experiment with colors and yarn thicknesses. When you have created a collection either enjoy them in your own home or tie them up with ribbon for an unusual dinner party gift!

Size

Each mat is 6" (15cm) in diameter

You will need

- Square of water-soluble fabric about 8" x 8" (20 x 20cm)
- Ball of 100% chunky wool yarn (I used Rowan *Big Wool* in pink)
- Fabric adhesive spray
- Water-soluble marker pen

Making the coaster

1 Cut a square of water-soluble fabric. Using a water-soluble marker draw a circle in the center about 3½" (9cm) in diameter. (Use a glass for a template.)

2 Spray the square with fabric adhesive and fill the circle with a spaghetti-like coil of yarn. Continue by looping the yarn all around the edge of the circle. Needle-felt in place either with a multineedle hand tool or a needle-punch machine.

3 Spray again. Then, starting in the center, wind the yarn in a coil on top of the spaghetti-like base.

4 Finish by tucking the end neatly under the coil. Needle-felt in place as for Step 2.

5 Cut away the excess water-soluble cloth. Rinse away the remainder in cold water and allow to dry before use.

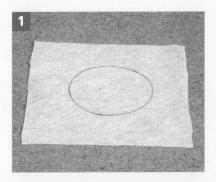

Braided coaster ideas

Try making these coasters with braided yarn for a more textured effect. Use several colors within each braid (see Braid-edged Jacket, page 56) so the coiled mat will become flecked with color. Use a single color yarn for the looped edge and the base. Needle-felt the braid in place from the right side to avoid the base color showing through.

check mats

These simple, very graphic mats are really easy to create. They employ water-soluble fabric as a temporary base, on which the yarns are laid down first one way, and then the other, to create a woven effect. The design here is simple and monochrome, but you can use the technique to make mix colors together, if you wish, in very subtle blends. These little mats are small enough to make with a multineedle hand tool (depending on how many you want to make and your patience) but are really quickly made with a needle-punch machine. They look great using either the right or wrong side—the latter has a more softened appearance.

Size

Each mat is 8½" x 11" (21 x 28cm)

You will need

- Water-soluble fabric 12" x 14" (30 x 35cm)
- Scissors
- Balls of 100% chunky black and cream wool yarn, such as Rowan *Big Wool*
- Fabric adhesive spray

Preparing the mat

1 Spray the water-soluble fabric with fabric adhesive spray (to ensure the yarn you lay on it stays in place). Cut pieces of black yarn to the width of the base and lay in horizontal rows, about 1" (2.5cm) apart. Hand or machine needle-felt to the water-soluble fabric.

2 On top of the first layer, create a second layer of yarn in vertical rows about 1" (2.5cm) apart. Repeat the needle-felting as you did for Step 1.

3 Now repeat the first two steps with cream yarn, laying each row in the spaces between the black yarns as shown and needle-felt as before.

4 Turn the work over to ensure that you have needle-felted all the yarns together.

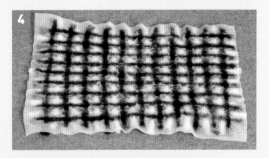

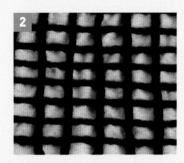

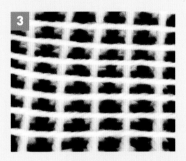

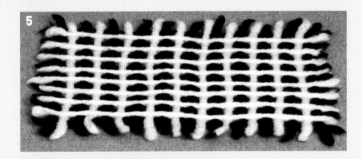

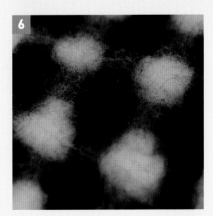

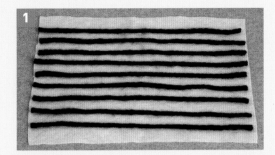

5 Immerse the mat in warm water to dissolve the water-soluble fabric. Rinse and allow to dry.

To finish

6 Finally, using a multineedle hand tool, needle-felt the entire mat lightly on the right side to fluff up the fibers.

alternative weave designs

The simple weave of the placemat inspired me to experiment with more intricate and colorful weaves and textures. As long as your yarns overlap and interconnect, the final fabric will not fall apart once you wash away the water-soluble fabric base. Interesting effects can be created purely by laying down yarns in spaghetti-like coils, which makes for quick and unexpected textures. I have continued to use thick wool yarns in most of these experiments but there is no reason why you should not try adding fancy yarns and strips of fabric to the mix! If you have a needle-punch machine you could make up lengths of fabric and produce unique scarves, throws, and garments. If you are daunted by the prospect of a larger piece you could also try using the technique as a fancy edging.

A A spaghetti-like coil of turquoise wool yarn was laid onto water-soluble fabric. This was then followed by another layer of thick cream wool yarn.

B If you lay different colors of thick wool yarn in a regimented order first horizontally and then vertically you will create a tartan effect. This fabric has a very loose weave achieved by leaving a larger gap between each length of yarn.

C By laying your yarns closely together on the water-soluble fabric the end result will look like a more tightly woven weave. This effect was created by first laying down vertical yarns in a pattern, the same pattern that can be seen on the front.

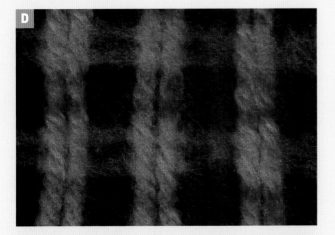

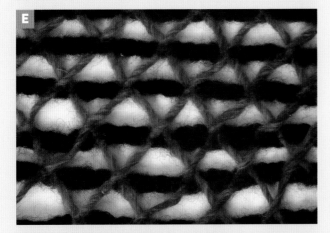

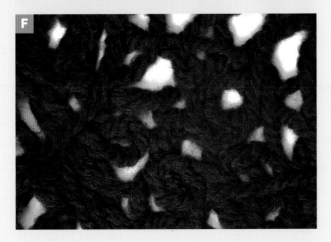

D A simple check has been created by laying down two hot pink yarns then two dark gray yarns and so on, in both vertical and horizontal directions. If you use really strong contrasting colors as I have done here, the results are really effective.

E This is where I started getting a little more adventurous! Begin by laying thick black wool in horizontal stripes across the water-soluble fabric, then add a thinner ocher wool yarn in a diagonal crisscross pattern.

F This sample was created by simply swirling thick purple wool onto water-soluble fabric. The interest here is in the pattern it creates like a kind of simple wool lace.

braid-edged jacket

Recently I gave a workshop on needle felting and had a sample with me in which I had braided some fleece and felted it to a background cloth. I think a braid is such a simple but beautiful thing and so easy to produce that the students started experimenting with the idea of using it. We discovered that, without a backing cloth, it was possible to turn the braid over and see the effect of the needle felting on the other side. The results were stunning—almost like a hazy mohair check. You can either leave one side as a more prominent braid or needle-felt both sides to produce a double-sided mohair effect. These braids have a multitude of uses: bag handles, braid edgings, and bookmarks being just a few.

This cream jacket already had a little detailing in the form of embroidery so I used this as a guide. The jacket is made of linen-mix fabric but as the braid is made of 100% wool, the fibers locked into the fabric securely, fixing the braid in place. The result is a jacket with a new look and a touch of Coco Chanel.

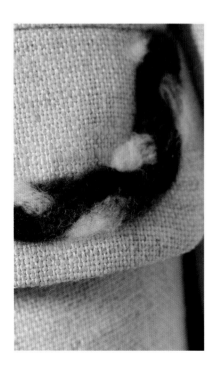

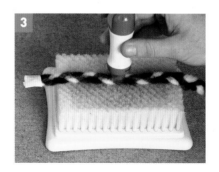

You will need

- Three different colored balls of 100% thick wool yarn such as Rowan *Big Wool*
- Water-soluble marker pen
- A plain jacket

Making the braid

1 Using water-soluble pen or chalk, mark onto your jacket where the braid will be applied. Measure how much braid you will need by following your drawn lines with a tape measure.

2 Cut three lengths of yarn, each a different color, at least five times longer than the measurement taken in Step 1 to allow for shrinkage when braiding and needle felting. Knot all three together at one end and tape to a tabletop. Braid the whole length and secure the ends with tape to prevent them from unraveling.

3 Needle-felt the braid either by hand or machine on one side only, as the other side will be needle-felted to the jacket and will not be on show.

Applying the braid

4 Needle-felt the braid in position on the garment following the marked guidelines. If you need to join lengths of braid, overlap the ends and needle-felt over the ends.

alternative braid designs

A   B   C   D   E   F   G

A Fancy threads can also be braided, but as I found in this sample, you will not always see the structure of the braid. I do wonder, however, whether that really matters when you have created such a wonderfully textural and unusual braid.

B I tried braiding with frayed strips of woven wool fabric, mixing open weave pink wool, a mustard tweed, and a cherry-red flannel. The needle-felting process flattens the braid and secures all the fabrics in place so that it will not unravel.

C To gain this more intricate woven effect, I used five wool yarns instead of three. This is one of those techniques that you think will be really confusing and hard but is actually really easy (see right).

D This braid is an alternative colorway to the one used on the jacket and is braided in the standard three-twist method.

E I had to try this technique out using silk. Imagine how pretty this braid would look if it was used for the straps on a floaty camisole top, for example.

F Braiding with two yarns rather than one creates a really abstract design on this braid. I used both a black and a white yarn for each segment of braid. Obviously the more yarn you use, the thicker the final braid will be.

G This braid was made using fleece instead of yarn. The effect is a really chunky, oversized braid in which the colors merge together beautifully.

Making a five-twist braid

1 Start off by cutting five lengths of yarn or fleece and tie them together with a simple knot at one end. Tape to a tabletop.

2 Start with one of the outer lengths—it doesn't matter which side—and cross it over the two threads next to it and into the middle.

3 Now do the same with the outer length from the other side.

4 Keep braiding, always crossing the outerlengths over into the middle and remembering to swap sides each time. Gently tighten the braid each time you cross over, pushing the braided section gently up to the last braid each time.

yarns on fabric

Simply laying down yarns and embellishing them onto a fabric can create stunning decorative effects, allowing you to create your own textiles and create new woolen pinstripes or plaids or dynamic and exciting decorative motifs.

Some of my most successful experiments have been produced using chunky 100% wool knitting yarn, as this needle-felts very quickly and easily. But all types of yarn can be used, from fine to chunky, plain to metalic—it is just a matter of experimenting and remembering that both the base fabric and the yarns applied to it need to be sufficiently fibrous for them to mesh together. Thinner yarns can be more time-consuming as it takes longer for them to adhere.

So many designs can be created by needle-felting yarns to fabric. It is a technique that can be used not only on items for the home, such as cushions and throws, but for your own garments, too, such as scarves or jackets.

daisy cushions

These cushions with their graphic floral motif will brighten up any home. Your friends will wonder how you created them without a single stitch! For a simple semi-abstract design like this, you need only to work out the center point of the cushion and then lay the yarns on the surface to create a doodle-like design.

A needle-punch machine makes short work of needle-felting such a design, but it is also simple enough to create with a multineedle hand tool if you don't have a machine.

Once you have finished the needle-felted design, you can make up the cushions in the usual way with a simple envelope-flap back.

Size

The front piece of your cushion will eventually measure 14½" (36cm) square but in order to allow for the needle-felting process I suggest cutting your square slightly larger (16"/40cm square) then trimming it to size before sewing the cushion together

You will need

- ½yd (0.5m) light wool fabric, cut into three pieces: one piece 16" (40cm) square for the front and two pieces measuring 14½" x 10" (37 x 26cm) for the back
- Fabric adhesive spray
- Tailor's chalk pencil and a pin
- Ball of 100% chunky wool yarn in white
- Bouclé yarn (medium weight) in white
- Cushion pad (16"/40cm square)

Making the cover design

1 Fold the front cover fabric into quarters to establish the center point; mark this point with the tailor's chalk pencil or a pin. Draw the main petals (using the pattern on page 106 as a guide) on the right side of your fabric using a tailor's chalk pencil.

2 Using a multineedle hand tool, lightly needle-felt the drawn petals in the chunky cream yarn.

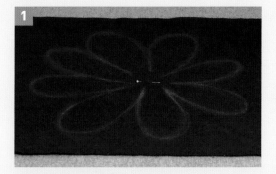

3 When you have completed the thick yarn flower, work two more flowers in a finer bouclé yarn, one inside the first flower and the other outside it. Make sure the outer petals come no closer than 1" (2.5cm) to the edges of your cushion front. If you go wrong, simply lift the yarn and reposition it.

4 Once you are happy with your design, needle-felt it securely in position either using the multineedle hand tool or a needle-punch machine. I always find it best to start at the center so that any shrinkage of the yarn will not affect the core of the flower.

5 To make up the cushion cover, hem the back cushion cover pieces along the envelope opening ends, lay the front cover and the two back cover pieces right sides together, with the back pieces overlapping each other. Pin in position and machine-stitch around the edge.

TIP
On the flower design, to achieve a good join where the yarn ends meet, rub the ends together between your finger and thumb.

throw

Plain throws and blankets can be found quite cheaply now, whether second-hand or brand new. They come in a wonderful variety of colors and just beg to be personalized with needle felting. I find a plain blanket is almost like a blank canvas just waiting to be brought to life.

This design couldn't be simpler—you simply let your tailor's chalk pencil wander to draw random lines at each end of the throw, then use the lines as a guide for needle-felting. Once you get used to working on such a large piece and realize how easy and quick it actually is, you can experiment with more intricate designs and motifs. I think a scaled up flower design taken from the one I used on the cushions would make a fantastic motif. Or, if you prefer, why not try an all over floral using flowers of different sizes?

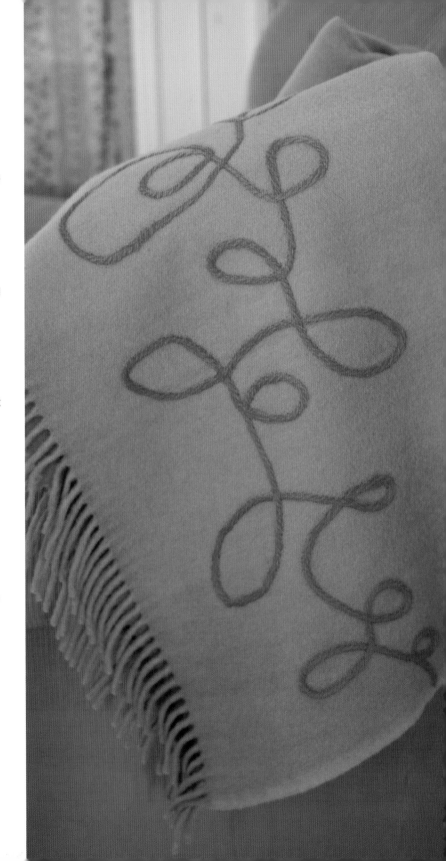

You will need

- Plain wool blanket or throw
- Ball of thick 100% wool yarn
- Tailor's chalk pencil

Steps

1 Take a tailor's chalk pencil, in a color that will easily show up on your blanket, and draw across one end in a scribble pattern. Don't worry if you go wrong, simply brush away the line and start again.

2 Using a single-needle hand tool, felt the yarn very lightly in position, following the design you drew. At this stage you can assess the design, move the yarn if necessary, and felt again if need be.

3 Once you are happy with the design, needle-felt firmly in its final position using either the hand tool or a needle-punch machine.

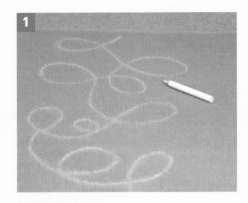

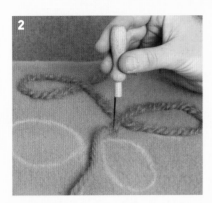

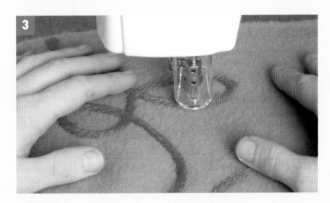

Adding a personal touch

Once you are good at needle-felting a flowing design like this, why not consider personalizing a throw with a quote or a monogram of your initials?

alternative patterns

There are many variations that you can play with on the same theme as the throw. Your design could be an all-over pattern for a cushion, perhaps. The major differences will be created by the combinations of different weights of yarns on different fabrics and whether you are opting for an all-over pattern or just an edging design.

I have experimented with a range of yarn types, from chunky wools to more delicate bouclé threads and even novelty yarns, sometimes mixing yarn types together.

Try to match the yarn type to the base fabric, perhaps using thicker yarns on heavier duty wool.

A Play with color to create stark contrasts and striking designs. A thick black wool yarn is used here on vintage orange tweed.

B This is on a dark blue background, using a specialty yarn worked in simple stripes. It would make a good edging for a throw or cushion.

C Bouclé yarns give an interesting texture to your designs. This swirl pattern on green felt could be used either as an edging or an all-over design.

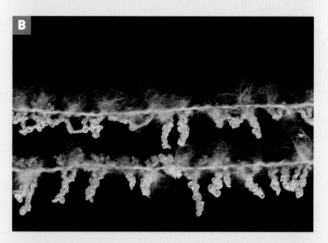

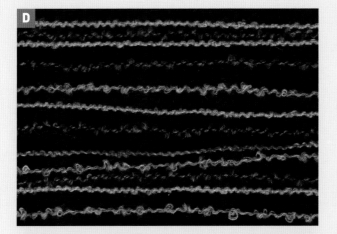

D This design is worked on black flannel and incorporates a variety of yarns and textures.

E This military-inspired design was created using thick raspberry wool yarn on gray flannel. It would work well on the edge of a skirt or jacket.

F I used a variety of yarns in this sample in order to create a needle-felted tartan. The first layer was a needle-felted grid using thick black yarn and the subsequent layers of white bouclé yarn felted between this grid. Further vertical and horizontal lines of black and white twisted yarn enhance the pattern.

fleece to fabric

This technique is almost like painting and, as you experiment, you will find the most intricate and even 3-D results can be achieved. Instead of brushstrokes, you twist, blend, and layer fibers to create designs. These can be worked freehand and chalked onto the fabric or you can cheat and use a base fabric, such as damask, that already has a design woven into it.

It is best to use a little fleece to begin with and build up the fibers gradually. I have seen amazing effects where so many layers of fleece have been added they can be sculpted with a single needle to produce almost quilted effects.

As always with needle felting, check the back to see if you prefer the more muted image that appears there.

I have used needle felting on its own in this chapter, but there is no reason why you shouldn't combine it with techniques such as beading and machine embroidery. Experiment and have fun!

laptop cover

It seems pencil and paper have been replaced by our laptops! I often find myself packing up my laptop and wrapping it in a spare piece of fabric to protect it in my bag. I had been given one of those black zippered carriers but that ended up at a thrift store long ago. It wasn't just the lack of style, or the fact that it screamed out to the world that I was carrying a laptop, but the fact that, with more than one bag, I am likely to lose the rest! Hence the need to make a laptop protector and one that almost doubles as a laptop disguise!

I rummaged through my trusty stash of tweed to find this gorgeous mustard-colored fabric, which worked perfectly with the bright fleece. Any durable fabric could be used here and though I have frayed the edges, it would look equally good using a felted fabric and pinking the edges for decorative effect.

You will need

- Length of wool tweed (see instructions for measurements)
- Tape measure
- Pins and sewing thread to match
- Tailor's chalk pencil
- Small amount each of orange, yellow, and purple fleece

Making the cover

1 Measure the laptop by wrapping a tape measure around the width and continue to allow for the flap. Next wrap the tape measure all around the length of the laptop, halve this measurement and add ¾" (1.5cm) to all sides to allow for seam allowance.

2 Cut the fabric using the measurements taken and hem one of the shorter sides. Using your laptop as a guide, fold the fabric to form the case and pin in place. Remove the laptop and, with right sides together, sew up the pinned seams.

3 Fray, trim, or hem the edges of the flap. If you choose to fray the edges, make a cut where the flap meets the main body of the case so that it lies flat (the scissors are pointing at the place to cut), then fray the edges one thread at a time.

4 Draw your design onto the flap using tailor's chalk using the template on page 106. Using a multineedle hand tool, needle-felt your design onto the fabric. (See page 18 for basic techniques on making fleece flowers.)

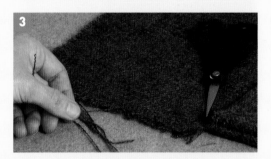

alternative patterns

Here are some variations on the floral theme I used for the laptop cover. You can use them as an alternative or they could be used for other purposes, such as embellishments on a garment or as a design for a book cover. All of them demonstrate varied ways of applying fleece, some using the fleece very lightly and others making a much more textured design.

As a textile designer I am inventive when it comes to finding practical sources of design inspiration. And I am always looking for ways to make my design life easier. Using an existing woven pattern, like the damask, or adding a splash of needle-felted color to a vintage floral print creates beautiful effects with relatively little effort!

A Iron-on embroidery transfers make an excellent pattern guide for needle-felting. Choose to fill in all the areas with fleece or leave some of the pattern exposed, as I have done here.

B A fabric that has a pattern incorporated into the weave as this damask does, can be needle-felted to give it color and texture. Simply use the pattern as a guide and fill in blocks of color as you wish. Highlight the design by needle-felting tiny rolled balls of fleece to form dots and by twisting lengths of fleece to form stems.

C When needle felting onto a base cloth it is possible to create wispy, featherlike designs. Tease and blend pink and orange fleece fibers before laying them onto a black felt base. Twist lengths of fleece for the stems and unravel the twist slightly, then fold under where it meets the petals.

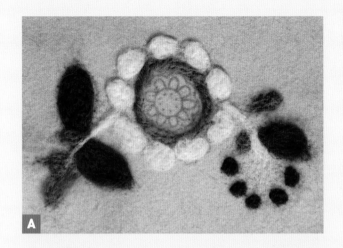

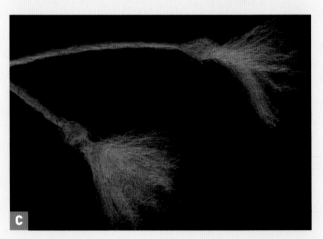

D Needle felting can be used to enhance and add texture to fabrics with a printed design. These simple turquoise dots of fleece were needle-felted onto a vintage print.

E I outlined these flowers first by needle-felting a light gray wool yarn to a thick gray marl felt. I then filled in the petals with purple fleece and completed the flower with a ball of light gray fleece in their centers.

F These clusters of neutral colored pansies were made using tufts of fleece that were a mixture of gray, beige, and black fibers. The background cloth is a light gray felt and the flowers were finished with little balls of white fleece at their centers.

G An alternative colorway to F but with slightly larger flowers.

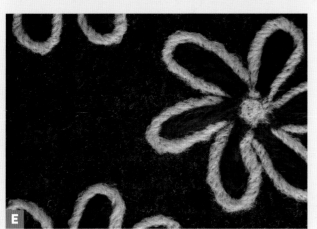

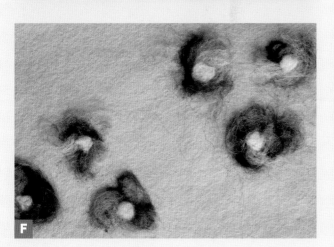

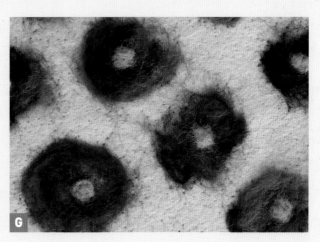

cookie-cutter sweater

Another great technique for applying fleece to fabric is to use a stencil or mold as a guide. Cookie cutters are fantastic for this and make light work of simple shapes, especially circles. All you do is stuff small amounts of fleece into the cutter and jab away with your needle! You can either work directly onto the fabric or make the circles first and then play around with the positioning before you needle-felt them in place. Of course, you could felt the circles more thickly and use them in their own right as buttons or beads. Whatever you decide to do with them, this simple technique is lots of fun and will have you searching the kitchen for different objects that you can use as stencils!

You will need

- Various colors of fleece
- A small cookie cutter or similar stencil or mold
- An old, plain sweater

Making the fleece circles

1 First make your fleece circles. I have found it best to use a single-felting needle and a sponge mat for this. Push small tufts of fleece into the cookie cutter and felt until you have a small dense circle.

2 When you have made a good number of circles in varying colors, arrange your design on your sweater and needle-felt lightly in place using the multineedle hand tool. This "basting" process means the circles can easily be removed and repositioned until you are happy with the final effect.

3 Needle-felt the circles in place using either the multineedle hand tool or the needle-punch machine. Put the sweater on, dance around to some loud music, and enjoy!

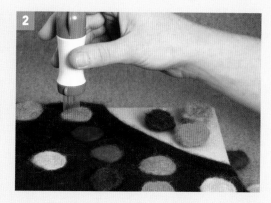

Ideas for other shapes

Little star shapes could be used on this sweater instead, strung around the neckline like a collar. Or make gingerbread man shapes for a child's sweater, embellishing details such as eyes and hair with little scraps of felt or fleece!

net flower top

Because wool fleece meshes together so easily, it can also be used to fix a nonfibrous fabric to another. It's like a type of decorative needle-felting glue and means that all sorts of fabrics can be incorporated into your work. I have a whole box of lace and net in my studio and loved the idea of putting these fabrics together with wool fleece as their contrasting textures look so good together. I hope this project will be just the start of your experimentations with different fabrics. Basically anywhere that would normally need to be sewn down can be fixed using this technique. The trick here is to begin to look at needle felting as though it were an interesting new form of stitch that can bind all sorts of fabrics together in a completely new way.

You will need

- ½yd (0.5m) of fine polyester net
- Water-soluble marker pen or tailor's chalk pencil
- Small amounts of fleece
- A plain top or t-shirt

Creating the flowers

1 Take a 20" (50cm)-square of net and fold it in half, then in half again, and press with a cool iron. Using a paper template taken from the pattern on page 106, draw a flower onto the top layer and cut out. Repeat this process to create four net flowers x 3 (or the number of separate flowers you require).

2 Lay the four net flowers onto the felting mat, moving each piece slightly so that the petals are not aligned. Take a small amount of fleece and using either a single-needle or multineedle hand tool, needle-felt in place. Repeat this process on the reverse of the flower to ensure all the pieces are securely bonded. Make two more sets of flowers.

3 Place the flowers in position on the garment and needle-felt in place using the multineedle hand tool, adding extra fleece if needed.

TIP

If you don't want the flowers to be a permanent addition to your garment, simply attach brooch pins or safety pins to the backs of the flowers with a few small hand stitches.

reverse effects

The reverse side of needle felting is often a happy accident, as you sometimes do not realize the effect until the project is finished. The reverse side has a much subtler look than the front, so that the fabric appears to be embossed or flocked. Once you begin to play with this idea, the results can be integrated into the design and the effect becomes a deliberate choice.

For good results, I try to make sure that each part of the design is needle-felted to the same degree. Results will differ depending on whether you use a hand tool or a needle-punch machine, and also on the direction that the needles take. The needles of a hand tool penetrate deeper, thereby giving a more fluffy, fibrous effect on the reverse whereas the machine produces a much flatter result. As always, do not over felt as this will lead to the fabric weakening and possibly to holes developing in it. And remember when reverse needle-felting, work on the wrong side of the fabric so the effect you require shows through on the right side.

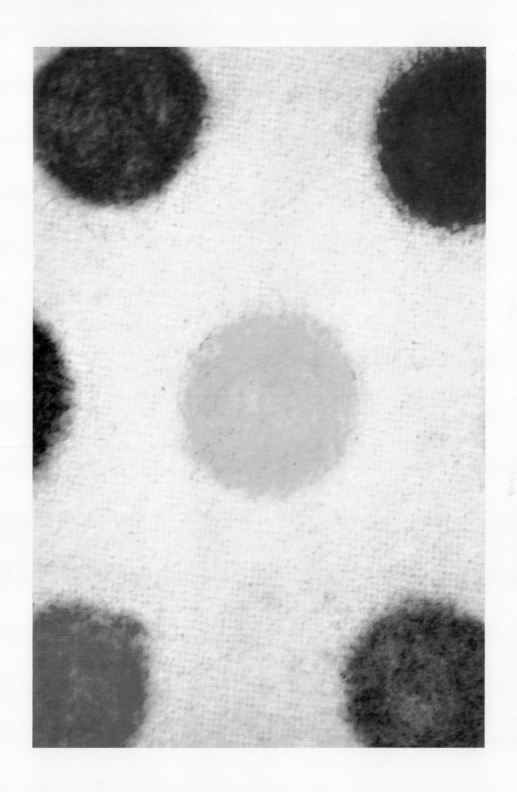

French press cozy

This simple French press cozy is not only practical but also offers a little textile "talking point" in your kitchen. The simple design is really easy to create and the fact that it uses felted wool means that there is hardly any sewing involved. Choose colors that compliment your kitchen so you can display it even when it is not keeping the coffee warm! The only tricky part when doing reverse felting is to remember what you have felted. On this design, I worked through the dots methodically. When working on the machine I found myself counting to 20 as I embellished each dot to ensure they all had an even amount of fiber showing through on the other side.

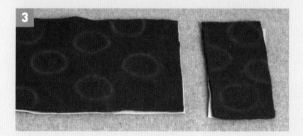

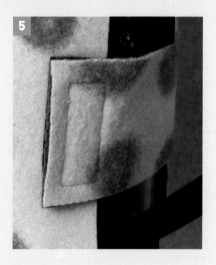

You will need

- To fit a standard 6-cup French press, two 7" x 16" (20 x 40cm) pieces of felt in toning colors
- Matching sewing thread
- 2" x ¾" (5 x 2cm) Velcro strip
- Tailor's chalk pencil
- Fabric adhesive spray
- Coin or thread spool (for template)

Making the circles

1 Lay the two pieces of felted wool down one on top of each other. Using a tailor's chalk pencil and a thread spool or coin (or other round object) as a template, mark your dots on the fabric. They can be fairly randomly positioned.

2 If you think the layers may slip, lightly bond them together with a light spray of fabric adhesive or a few pins. Now

start to needle-felt either using a multineedle hand tool or the needle-punch machine. Check the other side regularly to ensure that an even amount of fiber is showing through.

Making the cozy

3 When you have needle-felted all your circles successfully and evenly, cut out the pattern pieces. Cut the main body of the cozy to the depth of the glass area of the pot minus ¾" (2cm) and the width of the circumference of the pot minus 2" (5cm). For the fastening, cut a rectangle 2" x 1" (5 x 2.5cm).

4 To add the closure, pin the small rectangle of fabric to the center of one end of the main rectangle. Sew in position wtih a rectangle of top stitching. Wrap this around the press and check the

fit before you add the Velcro. Pin, then baste the Velcro in place, ensuring the cozy is a snug fit around the press.

5 Sew the Velcro by mimicking the rectangular stitch used to fix the closure to the main body of the cozy.

alternative spot designs

Layering two fabrics on top of each other and drawing on the design to be needle-felted is just one way to achieve reverse effect spots. If you want each spot to be a different color, for example, you will find it easier to cut out the spots in your chosen fabric and needle-felt them as separate pieces. Similarly if you just require an outline of a circle, then needle-felting a circle of yarn to the wrong side of the fabric will achieve the required effect.

You can also vary the amount of fiber that shows through on the right side, which is controled by how far you push the fibers through the fabric and how many times you punch. Finally, you can try needle-felting a single piece of fabric to create texture on the reverse—this works particularly well as shown here on denim. Remember that the wool yarn shrinks when it is needle-felted so it is important not to stretch the yarn when you initially needle-felt the design. If any fabric distortion occurs, press with a steam iron to relax all the fibers.

A These outlines were made by needle-felting circles of thick white yarn to the wrong side of a piece of gray marled felt. I applied them quite randomly with a deliberate slight variation in the sizes.

B To gain this multicolored polka dot effect, I cut circles from various colors of felt and then needle-felted them to the wrong side of a thick cream wool fabric so that the reverse effect showed through on the right side.

C This is another experiment with silk, this time backed with cotton batting. With this sample I first needle-felted both layers together from the front to gather and pucker the silk, and then turned the sample over and needle-felted it from the wrong side to push the fibers from the batting through to the right side to create the white fibrous dots.

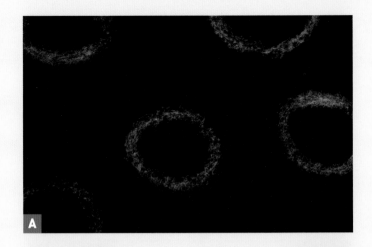

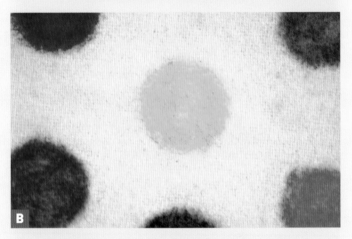

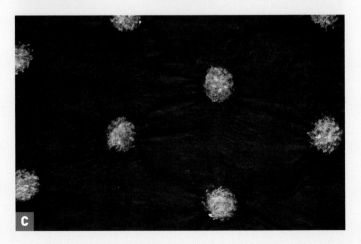

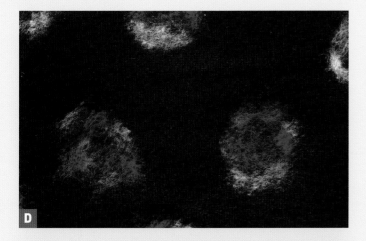

D To create a multitude of colors within one circle, you can either build up your circles using different colored yarns and fleeces, as I did here, or use a multicolored fabric on the reverse.

E Denim can be reverse needle-felted using no extra fabric at all. Simply needle-felt from the wrong side to push the white threads in the weave through to the front. Denim can also be needle-felted from the wrong side to produce deliberately distressed effects. Simply draw your design onto the back of the fabric and needle-felt your design. (This technique is really for those who have a needle-punch machine as I have tried it using a hand tool with mixed results.)

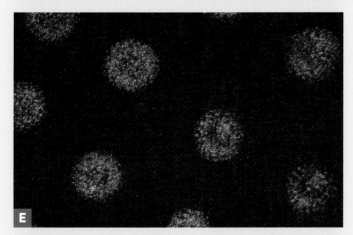

F The amount of fiber that shows through on the right side of the fabric will depend on how deeply you jab the needles. For this sample I used a multineedle hand tool to punch orange felt through a tightly woven red wool and then combed the fibers in one direction.

woven-effect scarf

This scarf combines the colorful look of fleece on fabric with the muted haze of fibers that appears on the reverse. Cutting the fabric in order to weave into it does not create a problem as the needle-felting process seals the cut edges. The weave is then needle-felted on one side, but only on the areas where the fleece shows, to prevent any of the ground fabric fibers from being pushed into the final design. The result is a reversible design that looks like a woven mohair. I like to use a checked or striped fabric so that the lines provide a cutting guide, but you can just as easily use plain fabric and mark the areas to be cut with chalk. Designs can be created that challenge the boundaries of traditional weaving or felt making, so experiment and be colorful!

You will need

- Check wool scarf
- Various contrasting colors of wool fleece—yellow, pink, orange, green, blue, and purple in this case

Making the scarf

1 Decide how you would like your design to look and cut the fabric at intervals accordingly. I made two small cuts at the intersection of each check. The easiest way to do this is to fold the fabric and make a small cut with a pair of sharp embroidery scissors.

2 Weave the first row of one color of fleece through the cuts, leaving it quite loose to allow for shrinkage when needle-felting. The ends of the fleece can overlap the edges of the scarf, as these can easily be trimmed away after needle-felting.

3 Weave your other colors through in the same way.

4 Needle-felt each fleece in place either by hand (as here) or machine. Needle-felt the exposed fleece on one side only, then turn the fabric over and needle-felt the exposed fleece on the other.

5 Trim off any surplus fleece fibers at the edges.

TIP
Be careful to needle-felt only the areas where the fleece is visible. Needle-felting over the areas of fleece on the underside will push these fibers through the scarf fabric, disrupting the design.

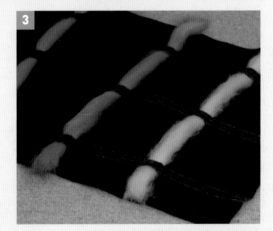

creating texture

The great thing about felting needles is that you can use them on fabrics that aren't usually associated with traditional felting and produce wonderful textural effects. I think I have tried needle-felting just about every fiber and fabric in my workshop. Sometimes nothing at all happens, other times you get a result: the fabric puckers, ruches, gathers, and frays! Organza, Chinese silk scarves, and chiffon all work really well with this technique. The barbs on the needle catch the fibers and pull them. This technique can be used to texturize single layers of fabric, and the effect gets even more interesting when you use a print fabric as the design also distorts. The fibers in these fabrics tend to be long and smooth—the exact opposite to the scaly fibers in wool fleece—and so don't adhere particularly well in an appliqué. This is not a problem with delicate items that don't need to be washed, but a few hand stitches, beads, or even a wisp of fleece will secure your work should you require a more robust finish.

I have included a couple of projects—a little lavender bag and a hand bag—but you can easily create throws and cushions using the textiles you create.

lavender bag

With all the wool around the house ready to be needle-felted it is important to keep the moths at bay, so I decided to needle-felt a little lavender bag, which you can hang in your bedroom or on a hanger in the closet. It creates a wonderful aroma, which fortunately the moths dislike.

The design is very simply made from a circle of organza that is threaded with a drawstring to form a pouch but, before you draw it up, you decorate the surface of the organza with texture and color so that it resembles a posy of flowers. These little bags are so quick to make that you can afford to experiment with the fabric surface and make different types to give as gifts. Add beads and embroidery for extra detailing or play about with color combinations. You could also add more petals to each flower by using several layers of fabric on top of each other.

Size

The bag measures 3½" (10cm) in diameter

You will need

- Organza 12" (30cm) square
- Water-soluble marker pen
- Various small scraps of colored silk
- 1yd (1m) of fine silk cord or fancy ribbon
- Tapestry needle
- Dried lavender for stuffing

Creating the bag

1 Using a water-soluble pen, draw a circle 9" (23cm) in diameter onto the organza and cut it out. Then cut circles from the scraps of colored silk, each measuring about 2" (5cm) in diameter. You will need about 20 circles for one lavender bag.

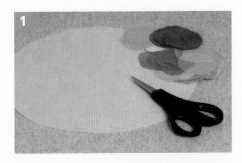

2 Draw another circle 5" (13cm) in diameter in the center of the organza. Attach the colored silk circles within this circle by needle-felting just their centers either using a multineedle hand tool or the needle-punch machine. Position the circles very closely together so that virtually no organza is showing.

3 Using a tapestry needle and fine cord or ribbon, sew running stitches all around the circumference of the flower.

4 Gather up the running stitches to form a pouch and fill with lavender. Once the pouch is nearly full, pull the gathering threads tight and knot to secure. Make a loop with the remaining cord and knot again. The lavender bag is now ready to use.

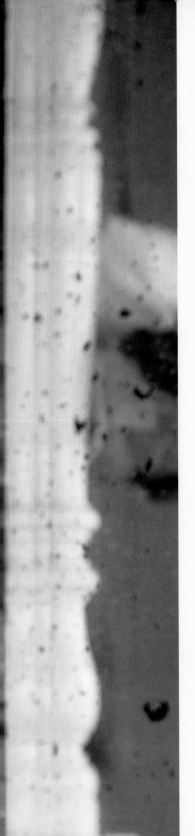

silk flower bag

My grandmother used to carry her knitting in a bag like this and, since I love updating old classics, I thought I would have a go at making my own. These simple unlined bags are really easy to make and the pattern can be adapted for any length or shape of handle. Many craft stores now sell bag handles, and vintage handles can also be found in a thrift store (although they may be attached to their original bag and this may well be far too beautiful to cut off!).

The flowers that embellish the bag are simply circles of silk that ruche up as they are needle-felted onto the fabric. The flowers will easily pull off from the backing fabric. I don't really worry about this with decorative, delicate items, but if the item needs to be washed you may want to secure the flowers with some invisible hand stitches, beads, embroidery, or a needle-felted fiber.

You can decorate your bag with as many or as few flowers as you like. The bag shown here is made on gray flannel with matching silk flowers, which looks quite sophisticated. The version shown on page 1 is in orange tweed with contrasting pink flowers—a more funky color choice!

You will need

- Pair of bag handles
- Wool flannel fabric for bag, two times the chosen bag length plus 4" (10cm) for the handle turnings and two times the bag width
- ¼yd (¼m) of silk for flowers

Making the bag

1 Fold over the silk fabric to create as many layers as possible. With a steam iron, press the folded square flat. Draw a circle roughly 2" (5cm) in diameter on the top layer. Carefully cut out your circles but remember they don't have to be perfect so if the layers of fabric slip a little it doesn't matter.

2 Starting from the center of one half of the bag fabric, needle-felt the silk circles in place either using a clover tool or the needle-punch machine. You can scatter them randomly. Make sure none are more than 4" (10cm) from the top edges to allow undecorated fabric for attaching the bag handles.

3 To prevent fraying, zigzag stitch the raw edges. Then fold the fabric right sides together and machine-stitch the side seams ¾" (2cm) from the sides, stopping 4" (10cm) from the op on each side. Fold down the raw edges to the wrong side and press, before top stitching in place.

4 Turn the bag right sides out. Slide one of the top edges of the bag through one of the bag handles so that the fabric on the wrong side measures 2" (5cm) and machine-stitch in place, gathering the fabric slightly as you stitch.

TIP

After Step 2, secure the flowers in place using a scattering of beads in the center of each flower.

alternative designs

Here are some different ways to ruche and gather one fabric to another using needle felting as the medium. The effects are quite varied and would work as entire textiles, or you could use them as interesting effects on accessories or garments. I think that silks bonded to wools are really great for these experiments, as I love the way the silk catches the light when it is ruched. This technique is really great fun to experiment with. The fabric can be worked as single or multiple layers or cut out and appliquéd. It is really a matter of finding fabric that reacts to the needles and then the gathering and puckering happens as if by magic! You can use this technique on its own, as I have done in this chapter, but it also looks fantastic when combined with beads, machine embroidery, and other textures such as fleece.

A This effect was achieved by layering deep red organza onto a similarly colored wool. The layers were then needle-felted in stripes, first on the right side to gather the organza and secondly on the reverse, to push the wool fibers through to the front.

B This simple but effective sample is simply made up of circles of polka-dot silk on a background of brown felt.

C Cheap printed chiffon scarves make an excellent source of fabric to play with. On this sample, I needle-felted some areas to distort the print and create a really textured surface.

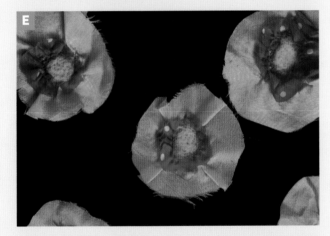

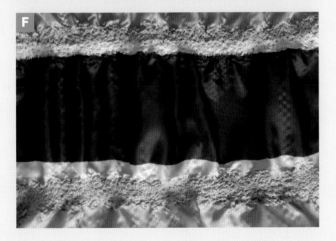

D Torn strips of fabric can be needle-felted to a background fabric to produce rows of ruffles. Far quicker than gathering with a sewing machine, this technique can be further embellished and secured by beading or a few lines of decorative stitching.

E Silk circles can be created with more than one layer of fabric. These have been firmly secured to the background fabric with a dot of yellow fleece needle-felted to the center.

F Another example of needle-felting a scarf. This time the scarf was a vintage striped silk one. I followed the stripes to keep the texture in keeping with the original design, creating an interestingly ruched effect.

needle-felting knits

When I was first introduced to the needle-punch machine I was shown a variety of samples to demonstrate the effects that could be achieved. Among them was a tiny piece of knitting of which one half had been needle-felted. It struck me as being so exciting to be able to felt particular areas of your knitting in a way that just isn't possible with wet felting.

I then started thinking about the different ways this technique could be used in conjunction with knitting. In this chapter, I have started to explore not only the possibility of needle-felting knits but also of using needle-felted yarn to create beautiful embellishments.

Once you have needle-felted a section of knitting it will no longer unravel, which makes it perfect for using as decorative edgings, as well as being used for "spot" needle felting isolated areas of knitted textiles.

needle-felted cravat

This little cravat was inspired by a vintage version that seemed to appear in virtually every rummage sale I ever went to! In the original pattern, the felted part in my version was a tightly ribbed loop; the cravat ends were formed into petal-like shapes.

Since my knitting skills are basic, I thought it would be fun to make a version that just involved knitting a simple rectangle. It occurred to me that if I felted a section of the knitting, I could then cut a hole through which the cravat ends could be pulled without the knitting unraveling. Also, I would successfully avoid all the tricky parts in the original knitting design!

Through trial and error I discovered that the cut area of felted knitting was not robust enough so I blanket stitched the cut edges to make a large sturdy buttonhole, which did the job much better.

To wear the cravat, just wrap it around the neck and pull one end through the big buttonhole.

If you are a better knitter than I am, you can experiment with more sophisticated stitches.

Size and tension

The cravat measures 27½˝x 10˝ (70 x 26cm). There are 10 rows and 9 stitches to 4˝ (10cm)

You will need

- Ball of chunky 100% wool yarn, such as Rowan *Big Wool*
- One pair size 15 (UK size 10) knitting needles
- Masking tape
- Tapestry needle

Preparing the cravat

1 Cast on 20 stitches and knit one, purl one, until the work measures about 27½˝ (70cm). You can make the cravat as long or as short as you would like, but just ensure you have a little yarn left over for hand stitching.

2 Bind off your knitting when the cravat is the required length. Mark where you would like your felting to be at either end. I used masking tape for this, as it can be difficult to draw an even line on a chunky knit. The areas I marked were 2½˝ (6cm) wide and 4˝ (10cm) from each end.

Needle-felting the cravat

3 Needle-felt within the masked areas using a multineedle hand tool or needle-punch machine. Work first from the right side and then from the wrong side until the area you have masked out is completely felted. If you are felting by hand, be sure to turn the knitting over frequently to help flatten the fibers.

4 Remove the masking tape. Cut a 3˝ (6.5cm) slit in one end.

5 Thread a tapestry needle with the same wool and buttonhole stitch (see below) or blanket stitch, all around the opening.

How to work buttonhole stitch

Stitch ⅓˝ (8mm) from the slit, as shown, loop the yarn around the needle, and bring the needle back down. Make subsequent stitches close to the previous stitches.

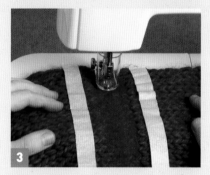

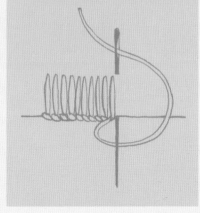

alternative felted knit designs

Here are just some different ways of needle-felting knits, but there are many more exciting ways to play with this technique, particularly if you are already a capable knitter. You can play with different colored stripes, as well as textures, and different stitches. You could also try your hand at needle-felting crochet if crochet is your thing.

Bear in mind, though, that needle-felting is a great way to revamp an old sweater that you have cut up, since the needle-felting secures the cut edges while also adding a textural design feature. Get creative!

A In this sample I felted the knitting in vertical lines, every other row. The effect is rather like an ornate rib. This would work well on a bag, I think.

B This sample shows how the needle-felted lines form horizontal textural stripes across the knitting. Obviously the felting limits the stretch of the finished fabric so be sure to take this into account when working your stripes on your finished item.

C I created the flecked two-color effect by knitting with two yarns together, rather than using just one. This technique limits the stretchy qualities of the knit considerably and changes it into a highly textural fabric.

D Dots of color were added by using the reverse needle-felting technique (see page 78), giving a subtly hazy effect. Small circles of dark green felt were needle-felted to the wrong side of the knit so that just the fibers look slightly fuzzy and quite soft on the right side.

E You can add color to the needle-felted areas of a design by adding different colored yarns to the areas that you are going to work. Here I have added a simple stripe by adding a single length of purple yarn to each needle-felted section.

F Here I have used needle felting to make an interesting edging design. I cut lengths of white yarn and added them during the felting process to create a false rib effect, which has a nice retro feel to it.

edged bolero

For this garment, I first felted an old wool cardigan in the washing machine. Once it was felted, I could cut it up without it unraveling. Any accidentally felted and shrunk sweater or cardigan can be revamped as a bolero, which means that it will probably fit you again!

For this design, I have taken the technique explained on page 63 and applied it to felted knitting. The needle-felted yarn design around the edges of the bolero is both decorative and practical, as it reinforces the cut edges.

I think it is rather fitting that this is my last project in this book as it demonstrates the fun you can have by mixing the techniques that I have described.

You will need

- Previously machine-felted cardigan or sweater
- Tailor's chalk pencil
- Dressmaking shears
- Ball of chunky 100% wool yarn, such as Rowan *Big Wool*

Cutting out the bolero

1 Using a tailor's chalk pencil first draw the shape of your new bolero onto the old cardigan. Check that it fits you and that you are happy with the design. To make rounded edges even, you can cut one side using a plate as a template and a pair of good dressmaking shears and then fold the cardigan over, so that the first cut edge serves as a template for the other.

Making the border

2 Take the end of your ball of yarn and loop the design along the cut edges of the bolero, lightly needle-felting as you go with a multineedle hand tool.

3 Once you have lightly needle-felted the design all over the bolero, including the cuffs, and are happy with the effect, needle-felt the whole design firmly in place either by hand or machine.

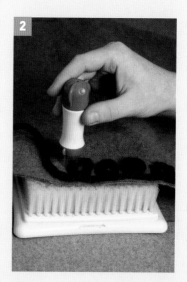

TIP

When needle-felting the cuffs, slip the sleeve around the needle-felting mat or if needle-felting by machine you can remove the flat bed of the machine (consult your manual).

alternative edging designs

Here are some different ways to to play with needle-felting edgings. A lot of these ideas have been borrowed from other chapters in the book, thus demonstrating the scope of these techniques. For example, adding needle-felted flowers to a sweater edge makes a really pretty trim for a child's jacket. Of course these edging ideas would look equally good on woven wool fabrics and could easily be used on the bottom of a skirt or the neckline of a dress.

A Create a decorative scalloped edge to your knitwear by needle-felting a wavy line of fleece to the cut edge, and then trim back the knitting behind the new edging.

B A bouclé thread was laid down in random swirls close to the knitted edge and needle-felted to secure. This technique is best used on very well felted knits as it does not seal the edge as effectively as the other samples.

C This fun edging was achieved using the flowers shown on page 18. Simply make a batch of flowers and needle-felt them to the edges of your garment. This would look particularly good on a little girl's jacket.

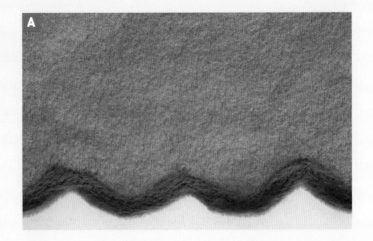

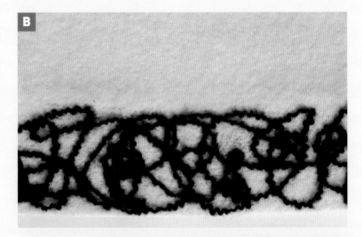

D I have borrowed a technique from the skirt design on page 32. This time the felt edging is based on the paper cut edging template shown on page 107. The purple felt used here stabilizes the edge of the pink knit so that it keeps its shape.

E This is a really simple idea for an edging. Simply loop your yarn half on and half off the edge of the knitted fabric, needle-felting with a multineedle hand tool as you go. The finished edge can either be left looped or the ends cut to produce a more fringed effect.

F This idea is basically a version of the one shown in the bolero project. In this case, however, I have also cut the centers of the circles and trimmed the edge around the border shape to give it a more lacy feel.

templates

Here are the templates which are needed for some of the projects. You can reduce or enlarge them on a photocopier to achieve your chosen sizes.

daisy cushions, page 62
laptop cover, page 70

floral cards, page 34
net flower top, page 76

felt flowers, page 40

snowflake table runner, page 30

border design (skirt border), page 32

suppliers

US Suppliers and Distributors

Coats & Clark
Consumer Services
PO Box 12229
Greenville, SC 29612-0229
800-648-1479
coatsandclark.com

Westminster Fibers, Inc.
165 Ledge Street
Nashua, NH 03060
800-445-9276
westminsterfibers.com

Pfaff
pfaffusa.com

Clover
clover-usa.com
Felting tools and mats

Ornamentea
509 N. West St.
Raleigh, NC 27603
919-834-6260
info@ornamentea.com
ornamentea.com
Great website with fleece and ready-
made felt balls for the really impatient
jewelry maker!

Yarnmarket
yarnmarket.com
Every conceivable type of yarn

Colonial Needle, Inc.
74 Westmoreland Ave,
White Plains, NY 10606
800-9 NEEDLE (800-963-3353)
914-946-7474
914-946-7002 (fax)
www.colonialneedle.com

UK Suppliers

Coats Crafts UK
PO Box 22
Lingfield House
Lingfield Point
McMullen Road
Darlington
County Durham DL1 1YJ
+44 (0)1325 394237
consumer.ccuk@coats.com
coatscrafts.co.uk
Felt, Filz-it felting wool and yarn,
haberdashery

Rowan Yarns
Green Lane Mill
Holmfirth
West Yorkshire HD9 2DX
+44 (0)1484 681881
mail@knitrowan.com
knitrowan.com
Big wool and other 100% wool yarns

The Cotton Patch
1283-1285 Stratford Road
Hall Green
Birmingham B28 9AJ
+44 (0)121 7022840
cottonpatch.co.uk
Needle-felting starter kits and specialist
yarns

Bags Of Handles
288 High Street
Walton
Felixstowe
Suffolk IP11 9EB
+44 (0)1394 279868
bagsofhandles.co.uk
Great selection of bag handles

Texere Yarns
College Mill
Barkerend Road
Bradford BD1 4AU
+44 (0)1274 722191
info@texereyarns.co.uk
texere.co.uk
Needle-felting tools, yarns, and fleece

Barnyarns
Brickyard Road
Boroughbridge
North Yorkshire
Y051 9NS
+44 (0) 870 8708586
barnyarns.com
Water-soluble fabrics, transfer adhesive

European Quilting Supplies Ltd
11 Iliffe House
Iliffe Avenue
Leicester LE2 5LS
+44 (0)116 271 0033
eqsuk.com
Distributors of Clover tools and brush mats

The Wool Company
Higher Hill Farm
Cardinham
Bodmin
Cornwall PL30 4EG
+44 (0)845 130 8015
enquiries@thewoolcompany.co.uk
thewoolcompany.co.uk
Plain throws and rugs

Pfaff
pfaff.com
Needle-punch (embellisher) machines

index

acknowledgments

We would like to thank the following: Anne Wilson for the design, John Heseltine for the styled photography, Luke Brason for the step photographs, Jayne, Ed, Natalie, and Gemma for modelling, Tessa Wilson for her location, Ed Berry for the diagrams and Katie Hardwicke for proof-reading and index. Thanks also to Rebecca Campbell for her help.

author's acknowledgments

Firstly, thank you to Sheila from Pfaff for sending me a needle-punch machine to "experiment" with. I must admit it sat under my desk for a few weeks until one day I started playing and thus this book was born! Thanks to Interweave for putting my ideas into print and everyone that helped along the way, especially Luke for being so patient and brilliant through the long hours of step by step photography! Last but not least I would like to thank my family and friends for their continual love and support.

Create Beautiful Designs

with these inspiring resources from Interweave

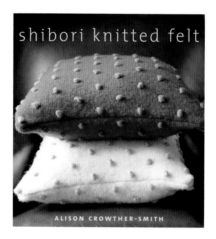